CONQUERING THE WAIT
A 30-Day Devotional

By
Kyndall Bridgers

Natoya,
Thank you
for your support!

Copyright 2020 Kyndall Bridgers

All rights reserved. No portion of this book may be reproduced in any form without permission from the publisher, except as permitted by U.S. Copyright law. The use of short quotations or occasional page copying for personal or group study is permitted and encouraged.

All Scripture quotations, unless otherwise indicated, are taken from the Holy Bible, New International Version®, NIV®. Copyright ©1973, 1978, 1984, 2011 by Biblica, Inc.™ Used by permission of Zondervan. All rights reserved worldwide. www.zondervan.comThe "NIV" and "New International Version" are trademarks registered in the United States Patent and Trademark Office by Biblica, Inc.™

Printed in the United States of America

ISBN

Published by: Awaken U Publishing Company

www.janayroberson.com

Table of Contents

Acknowledgments vi
Introduction vii
Day 1 Exile 1
Day 2 Safety 5
Day 3 I Have A New Attitude! 8
Day 4 You Can Do It! 11
Day 5 Trust The Process 14
Pep Talk! 17
Day 6 Look Up, Not Around 18
Day 7 Fill Me Up! 21
Day 8 Rest Easy 24
Day 9 War Cry 27
Pep Talk! 31
Day 10 Joy 33
Day 11 Why Wait? 36
Day 12 Peace…Be Still! 39
Day 13 Roll Call 42
Pep Talk! 45
Day 14 Crushed 46
Day 15 Conditioning Yourself 49
Day 16 Supplying Your Needs 53

Day 17 Loading… 56
Pep Talk! 59
Day 18 Rejoice! 60
Day 19 Mic Check 63
Day 20 Push Through 66
Day 21 Discipline In The Distance 69
Pep Talk! 72
Day 22 God Loves You 73
Day 23 Opportunity Costs 77
Pep Talk! 81
Day 24 Let It Go 83
Day 25 Curve Ball 87
Day 26 Clean Slate 90
Day 27 Cut It Off 93
Pep Talk! 96
Day 28 When It All Falls Down 97
Day 29 Heart Check 100
Day 30 What Are You Waiting For? 103

ACKNOWLEDGMENTS

I recognize and honor God for giving me the vision and direction to write this book. I thank Him for my life experiences; without them, I would not have the wisdom gifted to me.

I thank my husband for his encouragement and love. Thanks to my family and friends for their continuous support throughout my journey.

I thank each of my spiritual advisors who continuously pray and provide nuggets of wisdom. To each of you reading this book, I am grateful.

INTRODUCTION

Waiting for a change of any magnitude can be tough. At times, we may become impatient, weary, and even worried if our change doesn't manifest the way we feel it should. In these circumstances, how should we really respond?

Many times, during my waiting seasons for the call of God on my life, I found myself responding in ways that were unhealthy, frustrating, and sometimes inappropriate. I missed and delayed opportunities due to my negative responses during my waiting period. In fact, I found myself running in circles, repeating the same tests because I could not see things from God's perspective. I just wanted *out*! Despite the many devotionals, prayers, and Bible-reading sessions, I found myself stuck in a season I couldn't just pray my way out of. Little did I know, God was still at work shaping and molding me into the person He created me to be.

Thank goodness, that is the good news! God is still right by our side during our dry and trying seasons of waiting.

He equips us with every tool, person, or thing needed to withstand any obstacles in our lives.

For the next 30 days, we will explore the importance of seizing the opportunities that present themselves during your waiting season.

As you hold on in earnest for God's intervention, I pray you will identify a few areas of focus during your prayer time. May your perspective change as you wait.

I declare and decree that you will walk in a different light and receive the manifestation of what you have been waiting for. In Jesus' name!

Day 1

EXILE

In the dictionary, the word "exile" is defined as the state of being barred from one's native country. Fitting examples of this are found in the Bible when the Lord had to send His people (the Israelites) into exile many times to capture their attention.

Sometimes, we find ourselves in places where we feel as if, like the Israelites, the Lord is trying to capture our attention. I definitely found myself in that place. My life was a mess. My relationship with my boyfriend had just come to a screeching, yet, public halt. My job had high demands and low pay. My blood pressure was spiraling out of control. And peace was non-existent. I was reading scriptures, praying, and fasting. Yet, nothing seemed to work this time. I was drowning in my own mess!

As I tried to put the pieces of my life back together, God moved me to a location further away from my family, friends, and what I knew to be my life at that time. I was excited about the opportunity to move, but I still questioned the reason. I could not understand why God was taking me away from what I knew and felt to be home. Frankly speaking, I did not want to move. But being submitted to God, I knew I could not pass up the opportunity.

After moving and being in a completely different setting, I was challenged in every area of my life. It was a stormy season filled with trouble. However, it taught me very important life lessons. I learned how to handle opposition and how to maintain my peace in difficult circumstances.

As time progressed, my relationship with God was refreshed and restored. I found rest from the conflicts in my mind. I was no longer bombarded by thoughts and plans running around in my mind. Instead, I allowed God's plans into my life.

God told Abram,

> *Go from your country, your people and your fathers' household to the land I will show you. (Genesis 12:1)*

God had a plan for Abram, but he had to be removed from his current situation for God to execute it.

While David ran for his life, he sought refuge in many places away from his distractions. God was able to use him in ways he couldn't have created on his own.

In the same way, God used me in ways I couldn't have created on my own. Although I still had my home in my heart, I knew I would not return to that place until I was fully restored.

During your wait, God must develop aspects of you He may use years from now. They all have a purpose in His divine timing, not yours. In your season of exile, God has the perfect opportunity to get your uninterrupted attention to align your life with what He already has planned.

> *Consider it pure joy, my brothers and sisters, whenever you face trials of many kinds, because you know that the testing of your faith produces perseverance. Let perseverance finish its work so that you may be mature and complete, not lacking anything. (James 1:2-4)*

DECLARE IT

I WILL ALLOW GOD TO FULLY RESTORE ME
NO MATTER WHAT IT TAKES.

Day 2

SAFETY

I am reminded of a saying, "When the storms of life begin to rage in my life, I run into the Master's arms." Isn't it a good thing to feel safe? So often, we take safety for granted until danger comes. A hurricane is headed your way with strong winds and rain; a burglar has broken into your home and taken your most prized belongings; or, your significant other has abandoned you for someone or something else. Now, the immediate feelings you had of being safe have diminished.

The most reassuring thing in life is you can find safety in Christ. His arms are open wide, ready for you to run to Him as a child runs to his parent. He doesn't care how you got there, where you're coming from, or what you did. Like the Prodigal Son, He cares that you, His child, is now home...safe.

> *Come to me, all of you who are weary and carry heavy burdens, and I will give you rest. (Matthew 11:28)*

God is saying, "I know life gets tough. I know things happen, but you don't have to do it alone. Come to Me! I'll help you. I'll fight your battles for you! I'll give you rest for your troubles! I love you. You're safe right here with me.

> *Whoever dwells in the shelter of the Most High will rest in the shadow of the Almighty. I will say of the Lord, "He is my refuge and my fortress, my God, in whom I trust." (Psalm 91:1-2)*

DECLARE IT

I FIND REST IN THE LORD, AFTER ALL, HE KNOWS BEST!

Day 3

I HAVE A NEW ATTITUDE!

Society is constantly evolving, and it appears that if you're not keeping up with the latest trends, sayings, or people, you are not "in" with the crowd. Right?

On our journey in this life, we will encounter so many different influences outside and inside that can change our perspectives in an instant. If we're not careful or solid in our being, we can waver like the sea.

> *Do not be conformed to this world but be transformed by the renewing of your mind. (Romans 12:2)*

It all starts upstairs! As you wait for God to deliver you into your next season, you can be easily distracted by everything else. Hence, it is important to remain steadfast and unmovable in who you are. Remind yourself of who you are and whose you are. You may not have it all together right now, but you're amazing! You may not be at the same level your friends are on, but you are victorious! You may not have as much money as you would like, but you are worthy!

To remove the error of the world's way of thinking from your life, you must replace it with Gods' truth. It starts with you!

We are not defined by our status in life, our careers, how wealthy we are, our skin color or places of residence. Rather, we are defined by who we belong to—God.

Make a conscientious decision to believe and fill your mind with God's truth about you, no matter how long the wait.

> *You were taught, with regard to your former way of life, to put off your old self, which is being corrupted by its deceitful desires; to be made new in the attitude of your minds. (Ephesians 4:22-23)*

DECLARE IT

I AM WHO GOD SAYS I AM. I AM WORTHY, I AM VICTORIOUS, MY BLESSING IS WORTH THE WAIT!

Day 4

YOU CAN DO IT!

"That's it, you can do it! Keep going 5 more minutes. The results will be great!"

Do you ever self-talk to motivate and pump yourself up to finish a workout? Your body is physically wearing down and your emotions are saying you're over it! However, you're playing "mind games" to endure those last 5 minutes of your workout. And when it is finally over, you feel so accomplished.

Our physical bodies get tired and our emotions drained. Yet, we tell ourselves we can get through whatever it is that is trying us. In the same way, when you are faced with challenges, speak life into your situation. Although it may look dead and feel as if there is no hope, God has a plan. Until we arrive at that plan, constantly changing our mindsets will motivate us to get through trying times.

Your words have power, so your mouth will convince your mind, and your mind will convince your emotions, as well as your body.

Despite our weariness, we don't have to borrow energy from tomorrow or take a loan out on strength. God has equipped us with everything we need at *this* moment. Keep going. Speak life. You can do it!

> *Since we have the same spirit of faith according to what has been written, "I believed, and so I spoke," we also believe and so we also speak. (2 Corinthians 4:13)*

DECLARE IT

I SPEAK LIFE INTO MY SITUATION AND HAVE FAITH THAT YOUR WILL SHALL BE DONE!

Day 5

TRUST THE PROCESS

The unknown is scary. Having to move forward without knowing what's on the other side is frightening. Yet, with feelings of timidity, awkwardness, and fear, you reluctantly try to press on. In spite of those debilitating emotions, you believe God has your best interest at heart. Well, He does!

> *For I know the plans I have for you, declares the Lord, "plans to prosper you and not harm you, plans to give you hope and future. (Jeremiah 29:11)*

When the children of Israel were leaving Egypt, they didn't know where they were going, but they had to trust the process.

When God gave Noah instructions to build a boat in the middle of summer, he didn't know what would happen, but he had to trust the process.

When God told Sarah she would bear a child, despite her age, health, family history, and not knowing when this would happen (let alone at 90 years of age), she had to trust the process.

Power, growth, and strength are generated by going through the process. During the refining process, God builds essential characteristics within us, so we can excel on the next level of faith. God will never leave or forsake us. He supplies all our needs in the process. Therefore, we must release our doubts and continue to trust Him.

> *So shall my word be that goes out from my month; it shall not return to me empty, but it shall accomplish that which I purpose, and shall succeed in the thing for which I sent it. (Isaiah 55:11)*

DECLARE IT

I RELEASE ALL DOUBT, FEAR, AND NEGATIVITY. FOR THIS PROCESS IS ONE THAT WAS BUILT FOR ME BY AN ALL-KNOWING GOD WHO HAS MY BEST INTEREST AT HEART.

PEP TALK!

Making big decisions can be tough, Lord. There are so many options and it's a lot to weigh in. I don't want to make the wrong decision and create a setback. I need direction from You. You are my help. You are the source of my being. I don't want to lose sight as I wait.

Lead me through this time. Order all my steps. Teach me how to do life during this time. I forsake all my worries, concerns, doubts, past experiences, etc. I will rest in Your promises. I submit my request and decisions to You, Lord. I know You will take care of the rest!

Day 6

LOOK UP, NOT AROUND

One day, I was sitting on my balcony. I looked up and saw a group of 3 trees. The first tree was full of colorful leaves and very pretty. In the middle, the second tree was bare, with no leaves in sight. Then, the last tree had a few spare leaves on it. I thought to myself how can these trees be so close to each other, yet, each is at a completely different stage?

This immediately reminded me of relationships. People you may be in relationships with: friends, a spouse, or other family can be in completely different seasons than you. Like those trees, your relationships can affect your overall view of your season depending on how you look at them. If you view them from a carnal perspective, you'll believe the middle tree has nothing, while the others have something. On the other hand, if you view them spiritually or even logically, you'll see that each tree is at a different phase, preparing itself for a new season. It's all a part of a very necessary process.

How often do we look at others and compare them carnally versus spiritually? Our society has become very social media reliant. It is commonplace in our daily lives. Because of this, it's very easy to get caught up in what we see and doubt what we know.

God has mapped out each of our lives according to His timing. This includes when we get married, have children, start that dream job, or even complete a healing process. It may not be your season now but if God promised it to you, it is coming. Whatever it may be, keep the faith. Don't lose trust in God's process for your life based on what you see around you.

> *He said to them, "It is not for you to know times or seasons that the Father has fixed by his own authority." (Acts 1:7)*

DECLARE IT

NO MATTER WHAT IT LOOKS LIKE AROUND ME, GOD, I TRUST YOUR PLAN FOR MY LIFE WILL PREVAIL IN ITS PROPER SEASON.

Day 7

FILL ME UP!

Has your car ever been on "E"? It can make you a bit jumpy, especially if no gas station is nearby. "E" lets you know you have about 25, 15, or even 10 miles before you completely run out of gas. When you see this warning, you know you must make a decision. Stop everything and head for gas or take a risk and try to push it a little further. You may keep pushing from one place to the next. "I know my car," you tell yourself.

Car mechanics always warn not to ride on low fuel because it can cause long-term damage to your car. However, some of us ignore that warning and try to force our wills. We prefer to ride on "E" skeptical, nervous, and without peace when all it takes is a moment to stop, fill up our tanks, and continue to drive.

In the same way, sometimes we choose to ride on "E" in our everyday lives. "If I can just do this a little more" or "I know how much I can handle. I've got this under control." These are the words we tell ourselves when all God wants us to do is surrender and fill up our life tanks.

He knows what we are capable of. He knows what we can handle. He knows what's best for us. And in those hard, pressing moments when we are trying to push, pull, and tug on our lives to make it to the next destination, He wants us to surrender all to Him.

While we wait, it is important to remain filled so, we don't dread the process. Surrendering to Him and His will means you rely on Him to work things out, instead of trying to force our own agendas or control the situation. God knows we'll have troubles in our lives, but He wants us to be free from burdens with full tanks to continue our journey.

> *For I know the plans I have for you, declares the Lord, plans for the welfare and not for evil, to give you a future and a hope. (Jeremiah 29:11)*

DECLARE IT

LORD, I WILL LET GO AND LET YOU FILL UP MY LIFE TANK.

Day 8

REST EASY

Sometimes in our fast-paced lives, it is difficult to find time to rest. This can seem even more challenging during our time of waiting. Finding rest from our daily stressors physically, mentally, and even emotionally can provide much-needed relief to continue functioning properly. Our bodies and minds need rest to be restored. Numerous articles and books support this concept.

God designed us to take a day off.

> Then he said to them, "The Sabbath was made for man, not man for the Sabbath." (Mark 2:27)

God designed a time of observance and abstinence from work for Himself. How should we honor that when it comes to our lives?

We too need refreshment. In the new millennium, people are always "grinding" and overworking themselves to get to a particular level. But we must realize until God sees us as ready to elevate to our new level, we will remain in a waiting period—grinding. God desires and declares rest for us because it does not come naturally to us. Resting also takes a great deal of trust.

Trust God to continue to take care of you when you take the day off. Rest as a part of our weekly routine has been proven to help us operate more efficiently and perform better.

> *Six days you shall work, but on the seventh day you shall rest. In plowing time and in harvest you shall rest. (Exodus 34:21)*

DECLARE IT

I WILL TAKE A MOMENT TO REST, TRUSTING THAT GOD IS STILL WORKING ON MY BEHALF.

Day 9

WAR CRY

During battle, fighters shouted words or sounds to encourage one another or to frighten their enemies. This was called their war or battle cry.

In times of waiting, the Enemy will stir up frustration, bewilderment, doubt, and anxiety in you. It's hard to see through these moments but helpful to understand these three things:

  a) This is a spiritual battle
  b) We're not alone
  c) This battle is not ours

> *For we do not wrestle against flesh and blood, but against the rulers, against the authorities, against the cosmic powers over this present darkness, against the spiritual forces of evil in the heavenly places. Therefore, take up the whole armor of God, that you may be able to withstand in the evil day, and having done all, to stand firm. (Ephesians 6:12-13)*

This is not a physical battle. Your enemy is not your spouse, boss, or the lady in traffic who just cut you off. This is a spiritual battle. Your enemy is Satan. We must have the right perspective in war and be able to clearly identify the Enemy. When soldiers prepare for battle, they must endure intensive mental and physical training before they qualify for war. As Christians, we too must undergo training to be fully prepared for whatever we have to stand against.

Sometimes it feels as though God is silent in the times we need Him the most, but we are not alone. Rest assured He's always there. He will never leave you. The Bible does not promise us an easy life, but it does promise that Christ is with us, and we will never be alone.

> *Be strong and courageous, do not be afraid or terrified because of them, for the Lord your God goes with you; he will never leave you nor forsake you. (Deuteronomy 31:6)*

This battle is not ours.

> *Do not be afraid or discouraged because of this vast army, for the battle is not yours, but God's. (2 Chronicles 20:15)*

God is sovereign. He has the power to do anything, even the unimaginable. So it may appear as if you are surrounded by the Enemy with no way out, but take heart. Call on the name of Jesus. There is power in His name. Stand firm in your beliefs and let nothing sway you, even in times of constant pressure from this world. Make your war cry! You're not in this battle alone.

When you cry out to God, He will rescue you. He will send His angels to come and see about you. This is a battle. Though we may feel as if we're the only ones in it, it is not our battle; it is the Lord's.

> *The Lord will march forth like a mighty hero; he will come out like a warrior, full of fury. He will shout his battle cry and crush all his enemies. (Isaiah 42:13)*

DECLARE IT

I DECLARE WAR ON EVERYTHING THAT TRIES TO COME AGAINST THE PLAN GOD HAS FOR ME. GOD, YOU ARE MY STRENGTH IN BATTLE!

PEP TALK!

In the stillness of the hour, in the quiet times when emotions are high and confusion is all around, I find You in the serenity of it all. Lord, You are near; You are there. Even when I don't understand, even when I feel life and making decisions are suffocating me, You are near. Life is greater, much bigger than this trial I am going through. It is bigger than this sickness that is trying to keep me bound and this hard decision I am facing. Your words are planted in my mind.

> For I know the plans I have for you. Plans to prosper you and not to harm you, plans to give you hope and a future. (Jeremiah 29:11)

Lord, You see the entire picture. I can only see this small frame of right now. I am confident You've got me! Focus. Breathe. Be Still. Quiet the noise. Quiet the naysayers. Be still my emotions. Be still my feelings. You are near. You are here, and You care about me. You are involved in what I care about. Amid everything, I must be still to hear Your quiet, yet, still voice.

Day 10

JOY

Being happy can be contingent upon our emotions, thoughts, moods, and even perceptions. Although happiness and joy can be used interchangeably, the source of the two tends to differ. When we abide in Christ, He gives us intangible things to help us in our daily walks of life. Joy, which is a part of the fruit of the Spirit, is present even during the fiery trials. It gives us great delight, even when things are falling apart all around us. Joy can be our strength!

Growing up in church, I remember the older deacons saying, "You're either coming out of a storm or going into one." As a child, since I didn't really care for storms that saying scared me. I wondered when I would catch a break. How can I possibly be happy if I am always in a storm? What I didn't realize during my younger years was the joy that was counted out. As we grow older and wiser and have different experiences, we learn to appreciate and value things more. We view life through a different lens.

Although I am in my waiting season, my perspective is what can make or break me during my time here. The joy the Lord gives provides a layer of covering that can't break easily. It is not something that can fall apart when you feel you've been waiting on God for too long. It is not something that can crumble to pieces in the face of adversity. It is not contingent upon stuff or things. But it is deeply rooted, heart-filled, unexplainable in the most difficult times joy that will carry you through your journey. God wants each of us to have this. This joy will provide clarity and produce the hope and strength you need to keep moving.

> *Count it all joy, my brothers, whenever you face trials of many kinds, because you know that the testing of your faith develops perseverance. (James 1:2-3)*

DECLARE IT

IN AND OUT OF SEASONS, I WILL DECLARE THAT JOY WILL REMAIN IN MY LIFE.

Day 11

WHY WAIT?

"Time is running out!" "I'm getting older." "Everyone around me has this or that." Have you ever told yourself these things? We've all been there. But we must remember a few things.

God is making it perfect! It will be right for you and all who are affected by you. He will make it right for now and in this season of your life.

> *As for God, his way is perfect; the Lord's work is flawless; he shields all who take refuge in him. (2 Samuel 22:31)*

God is also making you stronger and building your faith. A process is involved in everything we go through. When God is taking us to a new level, we have to change—purging the old and implementing the new. This way, when we get what God has given to us, we won't destroy it. Moreover, being at a new level of faith requires a new level of strength.

> *And after you have suffered a little while, the God of all grace, who has called you to his eternal glory in Christ, will himself restore,*

confirm, strengthen, and establish you. (1 Peter 5:10)

God is making it amazing! He delivered a nation in a night. This is God! He's making something for you that you will love. It is customized, and you will know without a shadow of a doubt it *had* to be God. It is beautiful, and He will get all the glory.

So remember there is activity going on behind the scenes, God has everything under His control. Whatever we are waiting for God to bring about *will* happen. He just wants us to be completely ready for the big reveal. Hold on!

He has made everything beautiful in its time. He has also set eternity in the human heart; yet no one can fathom what God has done form beginning to end. (Ecclesiastes 3:11)

DECLARE IT

MY WAITING IS NOT IN VAIN.

Day 12

PEACE...BE STILL!

They say, "When it rains, it pours." I never knew this phrase had meaning in my life until I experienced a season of what I like to call "downpour." A downpour is heavy, continuous rainfall.

In this particular season, many things went wrong all at the same time; at least, that's how it seemed. Now, of course, this is a matter of perspective. Sometimes when you are in a pressing season, it seems as if one thing happens after another. A loved one dies; your car breaks down, and then your relationship with your spouse takes a hit.

Why is this happening to me, Lord? How will I handle all of this? Have those questions ever come to your mind? Well, God tells us to:

> *Trust in the Lord with all your heart, and do not lean on your own understanding. In all your ways acknowledge Him, and he will make your paths straight. (Proverbs 3:5)*

Many things happen in our lives that we will not comprehend. We will have to deal with several situations we cannot fix ourselves. But God is able! Trusting in His will and plans for our lives, not only assures us, but it gives us peace. In turn, this peace will cause us to rest or be still knowing that all is well. Now, "well" doesn't mean life will be perfect, but it means God knows whatever is happening and will continue to supply your needs even in the toughest of times.

When we do not have peace, we try to handle life's problems on our own. We don't include God. Instead, we put Him in the backseat and carry on with our lives. However, this approach often makes matters worse, and we end up needing God's help anyway.

Try His peace today! He has enough to give to all of us.

> *And He got up and rebuked the wind and said to the sea, "Peace! Be still!" And the wind ceased, and there was a great calm. (Mark 4:39)*

DECLARE IT

I HAVE PEACE IN THE MIDST OF EVERYTHING.

Day 13

ROLL CALL

Roll call — "Present! Here!" Thank You, Lord! I've been so busy just going through the motions I have forgotten to live in the moment. Ever been there? I was reminded of this when I was singing in church. The praise and worship team typically sang about 3 songs, and I had to lead the last one. It was a new song I was excited about but nervous at the same time. As we were in the middle of the second song, I realized I was not focused on it. I was singing; the words were coming out but the passion and commitment were absent. I was so focused on the next part of the program that I missed what happened in the present. Roll call!

If God calls your name or asks you to do something in your wait, will you be there to respond to the call? Will you be present?

It's so easy to get distracted or be so focused on the goal that we forsake where we are at this moment. Sometimes we create unnecessary work we feel will get us closer to our future goals. However, it causes us to decline or miss out on present opportunities.

I've lived several different places. I can remember after leaving each location there was something I wished I had taken the time to do, places I wished I had visited, or opportunities I regret not taking advantage of. As the saying goes, "Hindsight is 20/20."

Sometimes, we may have moments where we seize the day. But when they fade, we are back in the hustle and bustle. Life is a precious gift from God. And although we have many troubles along the way, God wants us to enjoy it. He wants us to learn how to be content where we are. While we are planning our goals and new adventures or even waiting for God to move on our behalf, He wants us to live in the moment. We have a mission to accomplish here on the earth. Yet, we should smell the roses while we can.

> *Even though he should live a thousand years twice over, yet enjoy no good-do not all go to the one place? (Ecclesiastes 6:6)*

DECLARE IT

I AM PRESENT IN THIS SEASON AND WILL BE WHO GOD SAYS I AM RIGHT NOW.

PEP TALK!

I am enough! I have a loving, supportive, caring God who can provide everything I need in its proper season. Though it may feel as if I am lacking; the world is caving in around me, or things are not going the way I intended, God still reigns supreme. He has just as much control over this season as He does the next. I will take confidence in that and have hope!

Day 14

CRUSHED

You've made a lot of progress. You've completed steps A, B, half of C, D, and most of E. You believe in yourself! God might not be saying much, but by faith, you decide to make the big move because the Bible says, "Faith without works is dead" (James 2:14). And it also says "I can do all things through Christ" (Philippians 4:13).

Then it happens. You are crushed! You're denied. How is this even possible? Why is everything so hard? You did everything right and made the decision to go forward (even when you didn't feel like it). Lord, You were quiet anyway.

Why does it feel like everyone else around me is moving forward, and I'm just stagnant? I've been faithful. I've been making the right decisions. What am I doing wrong?

Have you ever been there? Have you ever asked yourself any of those questions?

These are very valid emotions that can be experienced. But, we have to be careful not to fall into a depression. We must choose a different response with the power God has given us.

Respond to God's delay with faith, not doubt. Respond to the set back with victory, not defeat.

Although we may not understand at the moment, God's ways are not ours. Your delay does not mean you have been denied. God is grooming you in every way unimaginable so you can properly receive all He has in store for you.

Stay focused on the goal and remember how far you have come, not how far you have to go. Let's crush our fears and unbelief with faith and hope. These things won't happen right away. Slowly, steadily, and surely, the time will come when the vision is fulfilled. If it seems slow, do not despair, for these things will definitely come to pass. Learn the power of patience!

> *Let us not become weary in well doing, for in due season we will reap if we faint not. (Galatians 6:9)*

DECLARE IT

I WILL KEEP MOVING IN JESUS' NAME, NO MATTER HOW GREAT THE TASK.

Day 15

CONDITIONING YOURSELF

Have you ever seen or executed a boxer's workout? I love boxing, and I used to attend a boxing gym to workout. It was always interesting because, within the hour of working out, 40 minutes was dedicated to building, strengthening, and conditioning. The last 15-20 minutes were for "working the bag." This was done with a series of drills, punching, and combinations. I always wondered why it took so long to get to the part I came for: working the bag! The coach quickly informed me I was thinking about it the wrong way; the conditioning was the most important part.

This can also apply to our life's journey. Often times, we are building, strengthening, and conditioning before we operate in whatever God has for us. In our eyes, this can take the longest time while we wait for God to bring our requests to fruition. But we must condition ourselves for this next level that God will take us on.

We Have to Build

> *According to the grace of God which was given to me, like a wise master builder I laid a*

> *foundation, and another is building upon it. (1 Corinthians 3:10)*

Ensuring God is our foundation, we must build our understanding, knowledge, and relationships. This is important so that whatever challenges come in our lives, we will have strong support during those times.

We Have to Strengthen

> *He gives strength to the weary and increases the power of the weak. Even youth grow tired and weary, and young men stumble and fall; but those who hope in the Lord will renew their strength. They will soar on wings like eagles; they will run and not grow weary, they will walk and not be faint. (Isaiah 40:29-31)*

While waiting for God to move, we grow tired and become fearful. But our strength to overcome in those times comes from God. We should continue to use the tools we gained in building to strengthen us on this walk of faith.

We Have to Condition

> *Do not look on his appearance or on the height of his stature, because I have rejected him. For the Lord sees not as a man sees; man looks on the outward appearance, but the Lord looks on the heart. (1 Samuel 16:7)*

Heart check! We must guard our hearts. After all, everything we do flows from it. When we do so, we will be able to test and approve what God's will is—His good, pleasing, and perfect will.

Mind check! What are you thinking? Our hearts and minds must be conditioned in a way that is (a) pleasing to God (b) pure and honest (c) encouraging and uplifting. Our time is not like God's time. As we wait, we must properly build, strengthen, and condition ourselves. When the time is right, we will be ready for what God has for us and work the bag.

> *Above all else, guard your heart, for everything you do flows from it. (Proverbs 28:26)*

DECLARE IT

I WILL ALLOW GOD TO KEEP BUILDING ME UP FOR MY NEW SEASON

Day 16

SUPPLYING YOUR NEEDS

Have you ever heard the saying, "It takes a village to raise a child"? Being raised in a single-parent home, I always expected my relationship with the parent I lived with to be extremely close. However, that wasn't the case. Due to our differences, many challenges arose in our household. Consequently, I felt certain needs were not met. However, God allowed others in my village to help me in my times of need. If I could not get what I needed from home, God provided a way for me to get it from others in my village.

In these seasons of drought, I could only see what was in front of me and the lack thereof. But as I kept progressing through the season and even looking back, I saw God provided everything I needed to get through each moment.

Sometimes we see a very narrow picture of what is going on in our lives. We have these ideas and thoughts of how something should be when God has called us to look at it completely differently. That's why in Isaiah 55:8-9, He said,

> *For my thoughts are not your thoughts, nor are your ways my ways. As the heavens are higher*

> *than the earth, so are my ways higher than your ways and my thoughts higher than your thoughts.*

God sees the entire canvas of our lives. We only see a small glimpse of it. It takes a certain level of maturity to appreciate this. But take heart! God has given us the ability to think on spiritual things and what He wants us to consider.

If you are a fatherless or motherless child, if you feel alone and as if no one understands, if you are in your season of waiting and feel hopeless, remember God sees and hears you. He cares. The seasons we face are only temporary. They are essential to our growth and development for the next season we will encounter. Remain confident that in this season, God will provide everything you need. It may not come as you desire but take inventory, and you'll see exactly where He is.

> *But my God will supply all your needs according to his riches in glory by Christ Jesus.*
> *(Philippians 4:19)*

DECLARE IT

GOD IS HERE AND WILL NEVER LEAVE ME IN MY WAIT.

Day 17

LOADING...

As I waited in the dentist's office, I decided to do some things on my phone. I pulled up my email account, and it displayed the loading symbol while it brought all my emails up to date. I had no idea why it started to do this. I did not initiate it. However, as I waited for it to catch up, I noticed it was loading from the year 2008. Impatiently, I thought to myself, "This is going to take forever."

As I watched my emails load, I could see the subject of each one, along with the sender's name. When I read each subject line, it triggered memories of what was going on with me at that time. I thought of the times when I was struggling, on top, and in between. I thought about where I was headed, who was around, and so forth. These memories reminded me that if God got me through those times, He's the same God who could get me through what I was experiencing then.

Those moments of reflection rejuvenated my thought pattern and helped me realize that at the time, I couldn't see the ending of that season. However, in retrospect, I recognize it was all for my good. As each email continued to load, I began to feel the joy of knowing, "Yes! I am going to make it through this season!"

Sometimes we let the weather of our seasons dictate and determine our outlook. We forget about all the other times God helped us because, for some reason, this season feels different. Nevertheless, although it may feel or even be different, God is the same.

> *Jesus Christ is the same yesterday, today, and forever. (Hebrews 13:8)*

Understanding God is calling us to do, be, and think on higher levels, we must rest in the confidence that He will be there every step of the way. Every one of us can say God has done powerful things in our lives. However, when we are 6 months in our waiting season, when we have exhausted everything we know how to do, and when we have been continually disappointed in our period of waiting, what happens then?

I challenge you to reload your memory with all of the seasons God has brought you through, all of the battles He has fought on your behalf, and all of the storms He has calmed for you. Reflect on God's goodness in every area of your life. In doing so, you will regain a sense of gratitude and humility that will give you a boost to positively keep going in your wait.

> *Praise the Lord, my soul, and forget not all his benefits. (Psalm 103:2)*

DECLARE IT

I AM REMINDED OF GOD'S GOODNESS AND GRACE OVER THE YEARS.

PEP TALK!

OK, God! I'm learning to wait on You. I know it requires patience, trust, and faith. But this internal clock I have is ticking...loudly! It feels as if my plans are sitting at Your doorstep like a package You haven't opened yet. Help me believe! I need a reset button somehow. None of my plans can be executed in my power, so I am trusting You. In the meantime, I'll refresh my virtues during my wait: love, joy, peace, forbearance, kindness, goodness, faithfulness, gentleness, and self-control.

As I get older, I have more of a burning desire to accomplish my goals and attain a certain level of "success." This success will align with where and how You need me to be. However, I will continue to use my virtues as You have intended to ensure I am always ready to receive what You have for me!

Day 18

REJOICE!

Therefore encourage one another and build one another up, just as you are doing. (1 Thessalonians 5:11)

How is this possible when you are in the middle of a struggle? When I am struggling, it seems as if everyone around me is elevating to a new level—at the same time. Through my worldly eyes, the people around me appear to be moving up the ladder, but I am stuck at the same rung.

Through my worldly nature, it is harder to rejoice with others when I feel I can't celebrate myself. But then, the question becomes what is the purpose? Should we only rejoice with others when we are on the same level? Should we only be happy for one another when we are gaining something in return? Is this what Christ wants?

We have to change our perspective. This keeps us mindful we should not compare ourselves to others. The Bible says satisfaction comes from doing your best, not by comparing yourself to someone else. We are called to higher ground to encourage, uplift, and support one another in and out of season, in and out of struggle, in and out of cheerfulness, as well as in and out of times. We are free to bestow love and blessings on others, knowing that our blessings from God are assured. God trusts us with this duty. In your season of waiting, God is still blessing you.

So when your friend gets that new promotion she has been waiting for, rejoice! When your cousin has the baby she has been praying for, rejoice! When your boss gets promoted to a new level, rejoice! Any other response should be checked immediately and brought into submission. Reject those negative thoughts and replace them with positive ones of happiness for others. One day, it will be your turn!

> *So if there is any encouragement in Christ, any comfort from love, any participation in the spirit, any affection and sympathy, complete my joy by being of the same mind, having the same love, being in full accord and of one mind. Do nothing from rivalry or conceit, but in humility count others more significant than yourselves. Let each of you look not only to his own interests, but also to the interests of others. Have this mind among yourselves, which is yours in Christ Jesus. (Philippians 2:1-7)*

DECLARE IT

I WILL REJOICE WITH OTHERS DURING THEIR SEASONS OF TRIUMPH.

Day 19

Mic Check

Testing, testing, 1-2-3-4! Mic check! God was so gracious to leave us with His Helper once we receive Him as our Savior. He is the Helper who intercedes on our behalf, edifies, teaches, and empowers us.

Jesus knew His time on the earth was limited; therefore, instead of leaving us hanging, He provided a way for us to receive guidance.

> *I still have many things to say to you, but you cannot bear them now. However, when He, the spirit of truth, has come, He will guide you into all truth. He will glorify me, for He will take care of what is Mine and declare it to you. (John 16:12-14)*

That is God's promise to us. However, how often do we listen to the Spirit? We are in a constant battle with our flesh fighting off emotions and sin. We are learning and relearning ourselves and trying to do right each chance we get. But our Guide who lives within us desires to speak to us as well. Are you listening?

So many times, we attempt to do things "our way," which often leads us into never-ending cycles of nothingness. All the while, the Holy Spirit inside is tapping the mic, trying to get a good signal, so we can hear Him. God knew there would be difficulties, trials, and issues of every kind that we would face. Therefore, He sent the Holy Spirit to help us through these situations. Why not take every advantage of the opportunity?

The more we listen to the Spirit, the more we can hear Him clearly. The Spirit aids us in our Christian walk and leads us away from the temptations of this world. He gives us the power to bear the greatest burdens, adversities, and longest waiting seasons. We also become stable, develop the ability to be peaceful, and create peace around us. But, the less we listen to the Spirit, the less we can hear Him and the more we feel restless, anxious, and defeated. Tap into the Spirit today. Allow Him to speak to and guide you as you reclaim your life during this season.

> *But when the Father sends the advocate as my representative-that is, the holy spirit-he will teach you everything and will remind you of everything I have told you. (John 14:26)*

DECLARE IT

I WILL ALLOW THE SPIRIT TO USE ME EVEN DURING MY WAIT

Day 20

PUSH THROUGH

Planning a wedding is not the easiest thing to do. Sure, it's exciting and liberating at times, but frequently, it's full of stress.

From my experience, most doors I opened had a big, tall chauffeur named "Stress" smiling and ready to take me to my next destination. Although I was marrying the love of my life, the process was still difficult. It's easy to be blinded by the stress and worries of what is going on in our lives right now. I pray for wisdom in all situations, so I thought I had things under control, but in actuality, I was crumbling on the inside.

Often times, when God gives you something you've been praying for, it seems whatever it is comes under attack. If you get lost in the attack, you start to second guess yourself and God wondering if it's really supposed to happen, if you're doing something wrong, or if you actually heard God correctly.

God often speaks to me through dreams and visions. One night, I had a dream. It was horrible. It was mainly about death but so many other things were happening in this dream I was at the point where I was an emotional and mental wreck!

Abruptly, I woke up out of the dream and heard God say, "The Devil comes to steal, kill, and destroy." Then, it hit me! It's not me! (Thank God) This is so much bigger than me.

The Devil saw where God was trying to take me, and he was big mad! But I was going about this the wrong way. I was fighting with the wrong weapons. I was looking at this from the wrong perspective. I was pushing through this with the wrong force!

> *But when you ask God, you must believe and not doubt. Anyone who doubts is like a wave in the sea, blown up and down by the wind. Such doubters are thinking two different things at the same time, and they cannot decide about anything they do. They should not think they will receive anything from the Lord. (James 1:2-6)*

If I had allowed these different stress factors to control me, I would never have received what I asked God for. God gave me a glimpse into my future, but I doubted him based on what was happening in the present. If I understand my ways are not like His, then I must also understand even though I can't see how He will turn my situation around, I can stand firm in my faith and believe whatever He said will come to pass.

> *But if any of you needs wisdom, you should ask God for it. He is generous to everyone and will give you wisdom without criticizing you. (James 1:5)*

DECLARE IT

I WILL KEEP GOING AND PUSH MY WAY
THROUGH NO MATTER THE DISTANCE

Day 21

DISCIPLINE IN THE DISTANCE

Have you ever fasted? Fasting is abstaining from something for a period of time. It takes a great deal of discipline and prayer to give up something your flesh desires to replace it with prayer and faith. The good thing about fasting is we know how long it will last. When we're waiting for God to move on our behalf, most times, we don't know how long the wait will be. We may have some good days and some bad days, but we still don't know when God will allow us to get to our destination.

Sometimes we may feel as if God is the driver in the car we are riding in, and we constantly have to ask, "Are we there yet? Are we there yet?" But it doesn't have to be this way. Take advantage of this season of waiting in every way. Remember, this is training and preparation for the next level of life God is about to bring you to.

As we trust that God is doing what is best for us, we should stay focused on the goal and not be distracted by the distance. God is our Father. He knows what and when it is best for us. For the moment, discipline seems more painful than pleasant but later, it yields the peaceful fruit of righteousness to those who have been trained by it.

Get into God's Word. Learn more about Him and who He is. Every story and account helps you trust your driver even more. Keep your eyes on Jesus who never loses sight of this race.

> *It is for discipline that you have to endure. God is treating you as sons. For what son is there whom his father does not discipline? If you are left without discipline, in which all have participated, then you are illegitimate children and not sons. Besides this, we have had earthly fathers who disciplined us for our good, that we may share his holiness. (Hebrews 12:7-11)*

DECLARE IT

I WILL TRUST THAT GOD IS PREPARING ME WITHIN MY JOURNEY

PEP TALK!

It feels as if I keep trying and failing. I keep giving, and I feel depleted. My hope in this season is low! But You told me to be brave and courageous. I do trust in You, so I know I will find new strength. I will soar high on wings like an eagle. I will run and not grow weary. I will walk and not faint. My hope is the driving force to fuel my faith. My hope gives me the expectation that what I am believing You for will come to pass. I feel as if I'm on my last leg, but You told me You will give me a future and a hope. Things are shaky right now, but this is not the end of my story. You created me to live and be. Be the lender and not the borrower; be above and not beneath; be the light in a dark room. You promised this to me! So I won't be afraid, I will wait patiently for You.

Day 22

GOD LOVES YOU

During the wait, it may feel as if God doesn't care about you because, well, it can be quiet. You may think if you don't feel God's presence, He's not concerned about you, He has "bigger" things to handle or you may ask, "Why is He making me wait so long?"

Don't allow these misconceptions to shape your thoughts of how God feels about you. When we gain a true understanding of who God is from His Word and our personal encounters, we can rest assured that even when we don't understand His ways, we know for certain He loves us.

We are in such a fast-paced, microwaveable type of world. Everything has deadlines, timelines, and urgencies. Yet, we serve a God who operates on a completely different clock. While in my waiting season, I became weary, confused, and often questioned myself to see if I was doing the right things. I would have conversations with God asking Him why He was taking so long and if I was going in the right direction.

When I drifted into these spaces, God would send me little encouragers to let me know I was on the right track, and He loves me. Someone would treat me to lunch when money was tight; a friend would send me YouTube videos dealing with my situation, or God would speak through my pastor to encourage me. Unfortunately, I was so stubborn I didn't allow these encouragers to fully minister to me. I was consumed with thoughts about how long I was waiting and didn't see a glimpse of what I was waiting for. Yet, God continued to press and send more encouragers until well...I accepted.

God knew I was struggling and although the wait wasn't over, He brought me back to a peaceful place so I could be encouraged while I waited. We have a responsibility as God's chosen to walk in the light no matter what season we are faced with. Understanding God means that even in our wait, we know He still loves us. Therefore, we can sleep peacefully, talk confidently, and walk upright knowing our Father has everything under control.

God is not like man. His love is not conditional like ours can be. His very nature is love independent of our actions. He knows we will face many trials and exactly where we are in our walk.

Open your eyes. Has God sent you an encourager? Did you accept? If you are unsure, ask Him to send help today and watch how He shows His love.

> *I ask God from the wealth of his glory to give you power through His Spirit to be strong in your inner selves, and I pray that Christ will make His home in your hearts through faith. I pray that you may have your roots and foundation in love, so that you, together with*

all God's people, may have the power to understand how broad and long, how high and deep, is Christ's love. Yes, may you come to know his love. (Ephesians 3:16-19)

DECLARE IT

GOD HAS NOT FORGOTTEN ABOUT ME. HE IS STILL WORKING ON MY BEHALF.

Day 23

OPPORTUNITY COSTS

Every so often, it may appear as if God is silent, so we can have the time to use the tools He has already given us. There I was, a month away from marriage with no job in sight. My fiancé was in a completely different state and all of our family and life plans were to be in the same state he was in. I had packed and moved all my belongings to where he was, so the only things left were my clothes and me. Scary, huh? So to some degree, I felt as if I had been there before, and I knew how to handle the situation. But after exhaustively applying for jobs for 2 years, having multiple interviews and promises from recruiters without being selected, I was in a panic.

My human nature accessed my entire situation and continuously questioned my path. I thought I had to be doing something wrong. God is my homeboy. He knew precisely what I was trying to do and where I wanted to be. My spiritual side was telling me, "Don't let what you see affect what God has already told you. Have faith." However, it was not something I saw physically at first.

> *Now faith is the substance of things hoped for, and the evidence of things not seen. (Hebrews 11:1)*

To me, it was very clear there was no evidence of what I was hoping for. However, I know God and despite all odds, I knew He would make it happen for me. I knew He would! So I told myself I would just wait it out. However, within this time, I had multiple hints the Spirit was telling me to speak to my current boss about my plans to move when I got married. The thought of doing so petrified me. I knew all the odds were stacked against me if I had this conversation and could not see any opportunity with my eyes. I did not see this conversation going well. However, I made a decision to put my feelings aside, pray to God and go for it.

> *The LORD himself goes before you and will be with you; he will never leave you nor forsake you. Do not be afraid; do not be discouraged. (Deuteronomy 31:8)*

I had the conversation, and it was not as bad as I initially thought it would be. In fact, more opportunities were opened to me. If I was not obedient to God, I would have missed them. I had to remove the power and control of my job, boss, and situation. I had to put them back into God's hands.

It may seem as if we've done this before but that's okay; it can be a daily process.

As our understanding evolves and is operative in our wait, we begin to put faith to work. It becomes the confidence we need at different times. When this confidence becomes fully operational, it is trust. This trust, which can be seen as a full measure of faith, comes alive and works within our relationship with God. What is God telling you to do? Have you stopped fear from taking control? Don't allow your fears to cost you an opportunity.

> *Blessed is the man who trusts in the Lord, and whose hope is in the Lord. (Jeremiah 17:7)*

DECLARE IT

I WILL PUT MY FAITH TO WORK IN AND OUT OF SEASON

PEP TALK!

If you ask Moses, he will say, "He is the rock, His work is perfect, all his ways are just. A God of faithfulness without injustice, righteous and upright is he" Deuteronomy 32:4).

If you ask David, he will say, "The Lord is my rock, my fortress and deliverer" (2 Samuel 22:2).

If you ask Peter, he will say, "Now to you who believe, the stone is precious. But to those who do not believe, the stone that builders rejected has become the cornerstone, and, a stone that causes people to stumble and a rock that makes them fall" (2 Peter 2:7-8)

God, You are my rock! You are my source of strength in times of distress and evil. You are a solid rock. You are dependable, constant, and unchangeable in nature. Although I have ups and downs in life that challenge my stability, I am grateful that You remain constant.

Day 24

LET IT GO

Often times, we are so consumed with how long we have to wait for "it" to come to pass that we misidentify the obstacles and tests sent our way. As I winded down the planning of one of the biggest events of my life, while dealing with other issues, I was vulnerable. I was praying but not hopeful. I was speaking but a little doubtful, and I was fasting but not intentional. I believed God but my waiting time was so long it caused hopelessness to sink in.

I had a few accountability partners to help me stay focused but not everyone can help you through everything. With a few months left until my wedding, I had a huge disagreement with a friend. Now, normally, my friends and I don't have many disagreements. And if we do, we can forgive, understand, pray, and move on rather quickly. But this case was different. This friend held a grudge and to make matters worse, infiltrated the thoughts of others with her views.

Because of how this issue evolved, my first instinct was to just say "good riddance" and dismiss this person from my life. But instead, I prayed for my friend and asked God to restore my peace because this situation had taken all of it. After about a week of praying, God revealed that I needed to extend grace. Grace, Lord? But...I am not the one who is wrong; she is. And she is definitely not extending any grace to me!

Very quickly I realized my pride was in the way.

> *Bearing with one another and, if one has a complaint against another, forgiving each other; as the Lord has forgiven you, so you also must forgive. (Colossians 3:13)*

I got so caught up in this situation I allowed it to distract me from what I had been praying to God for. I wanted to prove my character to someone so badly when in truth, it didn't matter what that person thought of me.

> *It is dangerous to be concerned with what others think of you, but if you trust the Lord, you are safe. (Proverbs 29:25)*

Some disagreements may seem trivial, but they can cause much turmoil. Therefore, it is necessary to develop the habit of setting our eyes on things above, which are intangible and eternal. God wants us to forgive, extend grace, and even be kind to those who dishonor us. Allow Him to deal with the rest.

When we are waiting, God allows certain things to test us. These tests, if handled appropriately, prepare us for our next level. Had I not taken heed to the Holy Spirit, who knows what would have happened? I could have prolonged my waiting period. With the bitterness and pride I had from that situation, God couldn't use me at the next level.

A fool gives full vent to his spirit, but a wise man quietly holds it back. (Proverbs 29:11)

DECLARE IT

GOD IS DOING A MIGHTY WORK IN ME THAT IS PART OF THE PREPARATION FOR MY NEW SEASON.

Day 25

CURVE BALL

Just when I thought I had "arrived," life threw me a curveball. I had been waiting and waiting for a job, and right on time, God answered and laid one in my lap. But there was one catch; it was in a completely different city than I had planned. My entire family was set up and ready for my arrival, but I would be 2 ½ hours away. Instantly, I was confused and somewhat upset. How could God provide exactly what I asked but in a completely different package? So what did I do? I weighed my pros and cons. Of course, the pros outweighed the cons, but I still couldn't make sense of it. We were married now and should be living together in the same household. But taking the job would cause us to be distant, yet again.

Sometimes God gives us just enough for what we need at that time. I was so confused about my life that I forgot how I got there. I forgot how God was in the midst of it and created a path when there was no hope. How He completely took me out of a situation and placed me in a newer, yet better one after years of trying in my own strength. The picture didn't look how I felt it should, so I lost my confidence and obviously my memory.

I was reminded of the children of Israel who prayed and begged God to free them from Pharaoh. However, when that time came, and they traveled through the wilderness, the picture didn't look how they wanted it to. So what did they do? They complained and became bitter. Inwardly, I had started to do the same. I was physically present, but my heart was 2 hours away.

When God gives you an assignment, carry it out with an open heart and mind. All I could see were the obstacles, challenges, and difficulties. I did not expect life to be easy once my prayers were answered, but I would catch a "break" from its challenges for a while. I was shut off from the opportunities and the newness God was trying to give me in this season. After praying for God's help, He granted me peace. Bit by bit, I began to see the possibilities of being in this situation.

Like me, the pathway to your destiny may appear to be filled with obstacles stacked in front of you, but if you continue to give yourself to God, He will show you different things. Place our complete trust in God, no matter the situation, size of the curveball, or what it looks like. After all, these situations take us by surprise, not God.

> *You, Lord, give perfect peace to those who keep their purpose firm and put their trust in you. Trust in the Lord forever; he will always protect us. (Isaiah 26:3-4)*

DECLARE IT

HOW THINGS LOOK TO ME IS NOT HOW THEY LOOK TO GOD. I WILL TRUST IN HIS PLAN

Day 26

CLEAN SLATE

Do you ever find yourself going back to the drawing board to reevaluate your circumstances and where you currently are? Sometimes you have to take a step back to reassess your situation. But what I often find is that in those moments of readjustment, one major thing is often overlooked: forgiveness.

The Bible talks about forgiveness quite often. It deals with the rewards of being a forgiving person, as well as the consequences of not forgiving others. Sad to say, this concept can be overshadowed by our own pain, pride, and foolishness. But forgiveness is the key to healthy relationships with others and God.

> *And whenever you stand praying, forgive, if you have anything against anyone, so that your Father also who is in heaven may forgive you your trespasses. (Mark 11:25)*

It may seem as if you have been terribly wronged by the offender, and that person doesn't deserve your forgiveness. If you feel this way, remember you are unworthy of forgiveness, but God has forgiven you many times.

Harboring unforgiveness, resentment, and holding grudges, will negatively affect you more than the person you are unwilling to forgive. "Forgiveness is not for the other person; it's for you!" This is true in so many ways.

We must show grace and compassion for others by forgiving them of their wrongdoings. This cleans the slate, so our mental, spiritual, and physical health can be as vibrant as God intended them to be. Do you find yourself going in circles and not accomplishing your goals? Check your slate. Have you been waiting for what seems like forever? Check your slate.

God forgave us of our sins and because of His love for us, He gave us another chance to live when He could have wiped out the entire world. He continues to forgive us daily by showing His love and grace. Why can't we do the same for others? Forgiven people should be forgiving people. Clean your slate.

> *Then Peter came up and said to him, "Lord, how often will my brother sin against me, and I forgive him? As many as seven times?" Jesus said to him, "I do not say to you seven times, but seventy-seven times." (Matthew 18:21-22)*

DECLARE IT

FORGIVENESS IS A LIFESTYLE THAT I CHOOSE TO LIVE.

Day 27

CUT IT OFF

There was a tall tree in the middle of the forest. The tree had roots, but they weren't too deep. Then, God stepped into the picture with a long metal ax and cut the tree with one swing. This broke the tree in half, and its roots were no more. He then left the ax by the dead tree and walked away. The preceding is a vision God showed me through prayer with my spiritual mother.

For me, this vision signified the death of generational curses passed to our children. As I prepared for the arrival of my child, this was something that plagued my mind daily. However, God, giving clarity during this time, provided the mental relief I needed.

Powers and forces much bigger and stronger than we will ever be on our own exist around us. We can do nothing to stop evil from forming weapons against us, but we know who can stop those weapons from prospering.

> *For we wrestle not against flesh and blood, but against the rulers, against the authorities, against the cosmic powers over this present*

> *darkness, against the spiritual forces of evil in heavenly places. Therefore, take up the whole armor of God, that you may be able to withstand in the evil day and having done all, to stand firm. (Ephesians 6:12-13)*

God has given us the power and authority to cut problems off at the root. Even if you have been dealing with a difficult situation for years, it doesn't have to progress to this next phase of life with you. Be determined to take a stand and make amends. God is your power. Take the ax in His name and cut it off!

> *I am delivered from the evils of this present world for it is the will of God. (Galatians 1:4)*

DECLARE IT

I WILL CUT OFF ANYTHING THAT IS NOT CONDUCIVE TO WHERE GOD IS LEADING ME

PEP TALK!

I have had enough! I'm tired of worrying, planning, and thinking! Lord, I give all these things that are plaguing my mind to You. Take this; take that; take all of it! In exchange, You gave me peace and joy. Your yoke is easy, and Your burden is light. I will trust You even when I do not understand it all! I need the rest that comes from You. For then I know it will be right! You're in control. You are my hope and the answer to every question, worry, and fear I will ever have!

Day 28

WHEN IT ALL FALLS DOWN

When it was almost time for my next transition, I had multiple plans in place. I was waiting for the last piece to get in line. Then, that piece, the one thing I was so sure would happen came to a screeching halt! It was like when someone pulls that one Jenga piece, and the whole tower collapses. At that moment, I was sitting with a crumbled plan of my own. In my eyes, this was the determining factor, the route, and almost like the glue to the entire operation! Now what?! My life literally flashed before my eyes. Thinking, "Lord, I am trusting You! I have been leaning on You! Why would You allow this to happen?" But I had to stop myself in my thoughts because I had a decision to make.

When your plans fail, do you run back to the planner and Creator or do you crumble inwardly because of the heartbreak? I had to make a choice realizing that ultimately, God is in control of everything. Regardless of how I valued this piece that crashed, God is still in control. He is working on people, places, and all things behind the scenes. Just because we can't see it, doesn't mean it isn't happening. So that devastation, that crash of the "critical" piece had to happen. It was all a part of His plan.

We may not understand why, but it is still a part of His divine plan. It may not feel good, but it is all part of His plan. Ask God for wisdom today and trust that even when our plans fail, He's still in control.

> *Ask me and I will tell you remarkable secrets you do not know about things to come. (Jeremiah 33:3)*

DECLARE IT

THROUGH THE UPS AND DOWNS, I WILL NOT GIVE UP ON TRUSTING GOD.

Day 29

HEART CHECK

Have you ever noticed that while you're waiting for things to change, you become overly critical or slightly pessimistic the longer you wait? I dealt with this during my first year of marriage. I wanted to change some things immediately after we said "I do." Now, I understood we were human, completely different people, and we may have even had different goals. But I believed God brought us together, so it had to work—now!

While you are waiting for things to change, especially those you have no control over, it can be tormenting if not handled correctly. As children of God, we are called to be hopeful, pray, and have faith. But how do you deal with our emotions while we are in the process of waiting with no sign of improvement anywhere? I struggled in this area. I would pray hopeful prayers but speak doubtful, complaining words. In Matthew 12:34, Jesus said,

> *You brood of snakes! How could evil men like you speak what is good and right? For whatever is in your heart determines what you say.*

And Jesus was right, of course! I was praying, but each time I didn't notice a change or if it seemed things were getting worse, I would retract my words. Then I would focus more on what needed changing than the changer—God. All things considered, remaining hopeful and focusing on God was a lot easier said than done. However, there was a big difference in the outcome when Peter focused on the storm while walking on water compared to when he walked on water and focused on Jesus.

God is able. We can change our hearts and turn our attention to Him, rather than on our current circumstances. While we wait, let's be heart conscious so that our words reflect our inner beings. No matter how long it takes for the change to come, we can act in genuine hope and love and continue to get everything out of this season God has for us.

> *Let all who are spiritually mature agree on these things. If you disagree on some point, I believe God will make it plain to you. But we must hold on to the progress we have already made. (Philippians 3:15-16)*

DECLARE IT

GOD IS THE SOURCE OF ALL THINGS. I WILL REMAIN FOCUSED ON HIM.

Day 30

WHAT ARE YOU WAITING FOR?

As I was reflecting on the waiting period I was in, I took a deep dive into my requests to God. Within the past few years, I had a series of major life and faith events happen to me. Many things tested my patience, faith, trust, and hope in God. I realized that during these moments, He was building perseverance and my character into who He desired me to be.

In this season, I also took an overall view of what I was actually waiting for. Sure, there were things and desires only the Lord could fulfill, but I was sure I had felt this way a few times before. So, what was I waiting for? Was I waiting for God to deliver me, bring me out of something, looking for direction, or for the manifestation of something in my life? The truth is, there will always be something we will have to wait for. Then, when it happens, oh, the joy and relief that come when God shows us favor, yet again. Until we come upon another task or test, we are right back in our season of waiting.

So, what are you waiting for? Now, the Bible says in Philippians 4:6,

> *Do not be anxious about anything, but in every situation, by prayer and petition, with thanksgiving, present your requests to God.*

God absolutely wants us to come to Him about everything, for He is our Source. But while we are on our way to the destination, we must be careful not to miss the journey—the journey of healing, forgiveness, creation, love, etc.

There are vital things God wants to share with us, show us, and manifest within us along the way. We don't want to spend each waiting period lying dormant believing we can't fully operate until God delivers his promise to us. God has given us everything we need to be effective in this season. So what are you waiting for? Activate your faith. Activate your worship. Activate yourself in this season. Don't allow your focus to be so far into the future that you miss the present. God will come through, so rejoice now. God will provide, so take courage now. God will supply your needs, so trust Him now. Is your wait only about getting to the "next" season or what happens within the journey? Revamp how you wait on God today.

> *I am an overcomer and I overcome by the blood of the lamb and the word of my testimony. (Revelation 12:11)*

DECLARE IT

IN MY WAIT, I WILL BE COMPLETELY AVAILABLE TO GOD TO CONTINUE MOVING IN MY LIFE.

Made in the USA
Middletown, DE
15 September 2020